How to Hire the Perfect Software Developer

How You Can Evaluate a Software Candidate's Problem Solving Skills in Less Than 5 Minutes with 100% Accuracy

Dave Merton

Legal Disclaimer

This book does not offer legal or accounting advice. You should retain the services of a professional for these types of services.

How to Find the Perfect Software Developer   *by Dave Merton*

ISBN-13:   *978-1523403240*
ISBN-10:   *1523403241*

Introduction

Thank you for taking the time to read this book, you will profit greatly from the wisdom it contains. I am grateful to have personally developed these simple but powerful methodologies over the years, as it takes a lot of the uncertainty out of the vetting process.

I'm going to make you the following promise: You will benefit immeasurably from these methodologies if you faithfully adhere to them.

Why I Wrote this Book

The software business has the potential to be one of the *best* and most *financially rewarding* businesses in the world.

As a software provider, you are producing and selling an intangible product; However, where else can you sell the same exact *product* for the same exact *price* on the same exact *day* to *more than one* customer?

Nowhere! That's what makes the software business so potentially lucrative.

Every ounce of gold, silver or platinum needs to mined from the ground, refined at a refinery and then sold and delivered to a manufacturer. That's a lot of handling, and it cannot be duplicated.

Each time someone needs more gold or silver or platinum, more needs to be pulled from the ground. Precious metals cannot be copied from a command line or a dos-prompt.

Every ounce of oil needs to be drilled and refined.

Every chunk of coal needs to be mined.

Every piece of wood, for lumber or home heating, needs to be cut down, cut up, delivered and sold.

However, a single "piece" of software can be resold an infinite number of times. That's true recycling!

So then, why do so many software companies fail?

Even if you have the best *idea*, the best *funding* and the best *leadership*, you can still fail! This undesirable situation can be avoided if you are aware of the most likely cause.

The cause of failure, in many cases, is having less than elite software development resources in place.

The powerful and revealing methodologies in this guidebook will empower you to remove this hurdle *forever*.

Acknowledgements

This book discusses a very apropos concept for the business world – the concept is referred to as - "critical skills". Understanding exactly what "critical skills" are, and then understanding how to identify them in real world situations, is the foundation of this book.

Several years ago, I had never even heard of "critical skills" as a business concept. Like most other people, I certainly didn't understand how to apply this knowledge to the interviewing and hiring process.

The person that I learned this concept from is the amazing author and speaker *Brian Tracy*. He is one of the best writers and teachers *ever* when it comes to the disciplines of business success and personal growth.

I thoroughly recommend that you read his books as often as you can. Listen to them in the car. Play them on your computer or tablet.

Whenever I listen to him, I find myself immediately implementing a lot of the suggestions that I hear. BTW – A good number of these suggestions from Mr. Tracy have assisted me immeasurably in my efforts to write this treatise. (That's good news, because this information is desperately needed by those of you that must select excellent software developers.)

Although I have yet to meet this productivity guru personally, I feel that he has been a mentor to me. – Thank You, Brian Tracy, for your enormous contribution to the world of business!

Contents

Dave Merton

Chapter 1 - Why You Need This Book

The "Bad News" is that identifying and hiring the right professionals for software development positions has *always* been a challenge. However, the "Good News" is that this no longer needs to be true for either you or your organization. I promise you that if you make use of the key principles in this book, you will be able to *quickly* and *accurately* assess the abilities of *any* potential software candidate.

You already know how *costly* it can be to hire the *wrong* person. Got horror stories? No doubt you have either heard of, or even experienced firsthand, the pain and frustration after learning that the wrong software resources were put into place.

Problems can include wasted salaries, lost/compounded time and missed opportunities. In addition, there are the other less measurable (yet very costly) areas like strained customer relationships, irritated co-workers, etc.

This book will show you how to mine the very best software developers from the field, while sparing yourself and your team from most, if not all, of the needless problems mentioned in the previous paragraph.

So where did this information come from? Good question.

After spending the last two and a half decades in the software industry, I've worked on all kinds of projects with many other developers. This includes software consulting and integrations for two of the largest drug companies, full stack software work for oil companies, direct mail, small businesses and testing laboratories. After conducting many interviews, and then seeing the long-term results of those that were hired, I've seen what works and what doesn't.

Add to that a few years of teaching public programming classes because I love doing it. Lastly, dozens of my friends have been personally tutored as an introduction to programming. I've seen it all. The result is that I could conjure up a few simple but powerful techniques that reveal immediately if someone can figure things out.

Over the years, I have streamlined these techniques and thus have put together three different tests to screen a person's problem solving skills and abilities. These three tests have been for both hiring purposes as well as for training purposes for individuals who were receiving personal software training and/or tutoring.

This was a slow and partly unintentional process, from the aspect of hiring purposes. These three tests first started out as a touchstone for me to gauge a new student's abilities, so that I would know what I was getting into with them. However, these three tests have become so much more, as I will explain.

Before we go on, there is something that you need to know: My simple tests have *never* failed to work. They have empowered me to *accurately* gauge the abilities of *each* of those individuals (students and work candidates) **one hundred percent of the time**.

This is *not* an exaggeration. I am not blowing smoke. This stuff *really* works. - But don't take my word for it. All you need to do is try it once (hire a person that passes the tests) and you will be a believer.

Note: I have seen excellent results from strict adherence to following the techniques discussed in this book. The persons that were hired got up to speed immediately and constantly produced excellent, profitable work. What more could you want?

On the other hand, sadly, I've also seen what happens when a company decides to completely disregard the results of these techniques and decides to hire a person for a technical position anyway; even though the individual candidate had already demonstrated an inability to perform even basic problem solving skills. In these cases, the end results were not at all good and the hired individual would need to be summarily dismissed.

You need to trust the techniques, not your gut. Sorry, but it's true.

How would you like to be able to evaluate individuals with the same accuracy and precision? You will absolutely be able to do this after digesting this information; it's *simple*. We will cover not only how you can do this, but we will also go over the logic of *how* and *why* this system works. You and your organization will be able to trust and rely on this system, and you will quickly become believers.

However, before we jump in, let's just take a second to chat about what you are probably doing right now (when it comes to selecting software candidates) and why you might not be getting the best results that you would like.

What You Probably Do Now

Please read the sentence below in italics and see if you agree with it.

Important Note: When I say "agree" I do not mean that *you* specifically do this when hiring, or even that you *agree* that the statement makes sense. I just want to know whether you agree that this is how most people think on the subject…

> *"Most people that are hiring software developers want to find someone who has <u>experience</u>, <u>education/credentials</u> and <u>good communication skills.</u>"*

Well? Be honest.

It's true… most people that are hiring software developers do in fact want to find someone who *claims to have experience, education and communication skills.*

Now, this seems to make all the sense in the world, right?

I am going to drop a nuke on this way of thinking. It's folly. It's also the only logical way to think about hiring a technical person if you haven't come across a better way of doing it.

There is a better way to think about this. Yes, there is a much more enlightened way: You need to find someone who can *demonstrate the ability to problem solve.*

Would you agree with *that* statement? It is very different at the core because it creates a separation as to how you analyze a candidate's value. The raw ability to problem solve isn't just one category among many. It is essentially the only category.

The normal mindset is for interviewers to gravitate back toward things like education and experience, but trust me, as logical as this may seem, this methodology is broken. - If you don't believe me, let me ask: How's it been working for you?

So, while most interviewers do this, meaning they try to find someone with experience & education, it is not necessarily the *smartest* approach, but it is how many interviewers naturally *think and behave*. However, here is a brutal fact of life: If you think and behave in the same way as everyone else, then <u>you *cannot* expect different or greater results than everyone else</u>.

Most people that are interviewing an individual will try to find someone who sounds like they *know what they are doing*. (Duh…) Most everyone thinks like that. Why? Because everyone *else* is conditioned to think like that! It is certainly the course of action that seems the most obvious, so why wouldn't you do it too?

Let's call this mental condition "E.D.W.E.E.D."; It stands for *Everyone Does What Everyone Else Does*. This is, of course, until they know better.

It gets more interesting. These next few statements will rock your world. What I am about to describe to you is true of at least 99% of the people that conduct software interviews. - This way of thinking is pervasive in the software industry, due to the absence of a better way of thinking. - EDWEED

Here is the first shock statement:

Most people (without even consciously realizing that they are doing it) evaluate a software candidate similarly to how singers, dancers and comedians are evaluated by a panel of judges on the popular TV shows. (Let that sink in.)

Note: This model appears to work for today's popular television show judges, simply because the judges are not paying the performers out of pocket.

> ***"If you think and behave in the same way as everyone else, then you <u>cannot</u> expect different or greater results than everyone else."***

On the television shows, the three or four judges each rate the performer or team of performers. It's usually a rating scale of one to ten. The scores, as we know, of each individual judge are then combined to tally up a final score. The "winner" is the person or team that achieves the highest *cumulative* score, no if's and's or but's about it. This is typical and seems to be a valid course of action.

This is how it's done on these types of television shows. Scoring is similarly approached this way in the Olympics. Some teachers will even evaluate their students in a similar fashion.

Well, guess what?

We are *all* conditioned to score things this way. We "score" the people that we interview, and we do this without even *knowing* it. It's automatic.

So, is this a *good* thing or a *bad* thing? – Let's go on…

At the hiring software company, the post interview discussions amongst the co-workers start to kick in. See if any of this language sounds familiar:

*"Well, **Candidate 1** is <u>experienced</u>, <u>pleasant</u>, <u>well dressed</u> and seems to be adept at <u>communication</u> with others."*

*"Hmm, now **Candidate 2** is less experienced, not as good with people <u>but</u> seems to be <u>very motivated</u>."*

Dave Merton

What that translates into in the brain, without us even being completely aware of it, is that we are already mentally "weighing" the *combined scores* of the potential candidates.

Do you see it yet? It is such a natural reflex for us because it is how we've all been groomed.

Let's keep going…

*"**Candidate 1** gets a 10 for experience, a 10 for appearance and a 10 for communication skills!*

Yes! A perfect 30!"

*"Oh, but **Candidate 2** gets a 3 for experience, a 2 for people skills but then a 10 for motivation.*

Hmmm… that's only a 15."

We could go on, but do you see the trap of this "cumulative skill scoring"? It is rather anemic because it overlooks <u>the most important skill.</u>

As hard is it may seem, interviewers need to rethink, even mentally *renovate,* how they evaluate prospective software candidates.

Now, let's take these post interview discussions a step further:

Candidate 1 might have scored higher doing the scoring the typical way, but it leaves out rather important details like how **Candidate 1** is 55 years old, owns a huge home, has 4 kids, 2 in college, leases a new Mercedes SL and is going to require a LOT more compensation than **Candidate 2** who is 25 and just starting out.

Are you with me so far? Good, because we are still just circling the airport! Bear with me…

16

As you can see, you were still playing the judging game. How so? The minute I brought up income you were trying to *calculate* if **Candidate 1** would still be a better *value* than **Candidate 2**, but you were still keeping a running score of all the different skills! Bam! Bam! Bam!

This just happened in your head, right now. Admit it! That's conditioning! See how automatic it is? You did it when you were trying *not* to do it!

Would you like to know why? It's this simple: You haven't been exposed to a better way of thinking…yet.

A better way?

Yes.

Here it is: You need to identify the ***critical*** skills for the position that you are trying to fill.

Did you get that? Let me repeat it, because the entire rest of the book is based on this one hidden truth: You need to identify the ***critical*** skills for the position that you are trying to fill.

What is a critical skill?

A *critical skill* is one that must be present. A non-critical skill is one that is nice to have, but cannot make up for the lack of a critical skill.

Soak that up for a minute… Can you start to see why the "total score" methodology that everyone gravitates toward is less effective? It doesn't take into account the skills that are "must have" compared to the ones that are merely "desirable". That's the key.

Learning this one truth will save you so much heartache, and will pay huge rewards in profitability.

Once you have identified the critical skills that you are looking for, then you will be much better prepared to find the individual that you are looking for.

You need to get this.

The best way to illustrate the difference between a ***critical skill*** and a ***non-critical skill*** is to provide some obvious examples.

You will see a list of specific skills for specific types of employment. In each of these examples, although there will be three skills listed, only one specific skill will actually be a critical skill. See if you can pick out which one specific skill is the critical skill for each job type. - This may seem ridiculously simple, but please bear with me – especially if this is a new way of thinking for you.

Example Job 1: Interpreter - French to English

Skills:

- Good manners
- Friendly demeanor
- Fluent in French and English

It's probably not hard to figure this one out. No matter how nice you are, you simply cannot do this job unless you are fluent in both French and English, period. The fluency is a ***critical*** skill. Good manners are important, but not critical. Why? *Because no amount of good manners will make up for someone who is not fluent in French and English.* Not having a critical skill is a deal breaker.

The main skill set to be assessing when interviewing a candidate for being a French to English interpreter would then be what? Duh... fluency in French and English.

> *"A critical skill is one that must be present. A non-critical skill is one that is nice to have, but cannot make up for the lack of a critical skill."*

Okay, that example was easy because it was so obvious.

This next example is even more so...

Example Job 2: Airline Pilot

Skills:

- Likes to travel
- Has the really cool captain voice when using intercom.
- Can fly a plane

Would you *ever* hire someone for this job by totaling up the individual scores from each specific skill in your head? No way, no how!

The reason should be obvious: Being able to fly a plane supersedes <u>all other skills</u> imaginable in this example. The ability to pilot an aircraft is ***critical***, having the cool voice is *not*.

The coolest voice in the world cannot make up for not being able to fly, however the inevitable announcement that would ensue would be one for the news programs. "But he sounded do *cooool!*"

Why isn't this approach used with hiring software professionals? Because no one has really thought it through, yet. - EDWEED

Okay, now we're finally getting somewhere. So, the big question is: What is/are the *critical* skills for a top-notch software developer? Only one of the skills listed below is critical. Fight off your mental conditioning and identify the one critical skill from the list below:

Example Job 3: Software Developer

Skills:

- Experienced
- Has eighteen years of college
- Can problem solve

Dave Merton

If you didn't pick "Can problem solve" then my guess is that you haven't been very happy or profitable with the persons that you've hired in the past.

Problem solving ability is the one, first, biggest **_critical_** skill for software development. Everything else, and I mean _everything_ else, is secondary. No amount of experience, education or shmoozability can make up for weak problem solving skills. (Not even a pony tail or a Microsoft tee shirt will make up the difference.) This is the sum total of what you need to understand before we go forward.

Can you see why experience and professionalism are great, but they can never make up for a deficiency in the **_critical_** skill of problem solving?

Maybe the individual could do sales, or worse, project management, but not software development.

If this is how you have been interviewing people in the past, don't feel bad. It's probably how you have been conditioned. This is especially true if you are perhaps the first technical interviewer in a series of interviewers. (Borg designation: 1 of 3)

You've probably asked the person what they've done already and then even asked them a few of the typical technical questions like:

"Where would you put a piece of code to execute right when the application starts?"

...or, even more common...

"How would you write a small function to reverse a string?"

Do either of these questions sound familiar? If they are questions that you've used in the past, do they still make sense to keep using? Who

20

possibly couldn't answer those questions? They are so "Hello World" it's not even funny.

This is the old way, and the old way doesn't work.

Why 'What You Do Now' Doesn't Work

Do either of those questions in the last section sound familiar? The second one will only tell you if a person understands loops and then a few of the most common functions for dealing with strings. That's rudimentary. How has that worked for you thus far in finding the perfect developer?

What you should be doing instead is seeing if this person can *problem solve*. Problem solving ability must be tested *apart* from any kind of software and/or programming language. It needs to be a little more *abstract*.

Why?

Because the ability to problem solve is like using a mental muscle, just like lifting a heavy object is a function of using one or more physical muscles. It doesn't matter what you are lifting physically, strength is strength. The ability to problem solve is also its own measurable skill, *separate* and *distinct* from the specific problem solving task at hand.

This book will discuss the three most important *dimensions* of problem solving. You only need to use the first two, the last one is more for your own purposes, meaning this: The first two dimensions will tell you if the candidate can problem solve, and you will have your definitive answer right there and then. The third test will give you an idea of just how mentally powerful the potential software candidate is, over and above being an excellent candidate. (Elite versus super-elite)

The third test is seldom given, since very few people ever get that far. Either of the first two tests are show stoppers in my mind, if the person fails.

Note: When you are introduced to the three tests, and you understand how they work, and which problem solving dimensions they are assessing, you will never go back to the old ways of interviewing candidates.

The third test is more for bragging rights. By the time I get to question three with someone (and this tends to be a *very rare occurrence*) I already know that I want them. The first time that you experience this exact feeling for yourself you will feel seriously empowered. Own it.

What I am about to say next is going to probably shock you, but it needs to be said. *Anyone* **who is in the software business should be able to pass *both* the first and second test.** It's *that* simple. The tests are simple as you will see. However, I am constantly astonished by seeing just how many "software" people there are out there that cannot even solve these *simple* puzzles. Believe me, you too will be astounded.

What is terrifying is that out of all the potential candidates that I have interviewed over the years, less than thirty percent of them have been able to pass the first two tests. (You read that correctly, the amount of software candidates who pass these three tests are less than thirty percent!)

Many of the candidates above, the 70% that fail either of the first two tests, are seasoned software developers, not just kids in high school. Does this scare you? If not, it will when you see what the tests look like.

Personally, I find that fact very disturbing because it means that there are potentially thousands upon thousands of "alleged" software development professionals that are gainfully employed in the software industry that are less than adequately qualified. Each of these software development professionals should have to be tested immediately for the ability to problem solve. - I'm serious about this. Someone needs to pass a law.

In your organization, that person is you.

...

22

So, are you ready to turn the software world as you know it upside down?

Glad to hear it! Let's get started!

Chapter 2 - *The Coin Test*

This chapter is going to be broken down into the following three logical sections:

1. How to administer the *Coin Test*
2. What the *Coin Test* is testing
3. Why the *Coin Test* is important

Each section will be covered below in more detail.

There will be a fourth "bonus section" at the end:

1. One for the Ladies

How to Administer the Coin Test

What you will be explaining to the potential candidate is that you will be giving them a certain "dollar amount". When you do, they must then come up with a total of three coins (not two, not four, but exactly three coins) that total the given "dollar amount". They may use any combination of nickels, dimes and quarters. The only requirement is that they must use three and only three coins.

Note: It is imperative that you clearly explain the rules before starting this test. Just to repeat them:

1. Three coins; no more, no less.
2. Nickels, dimes and quarters only.

What you will then do is give them an example to break the ice. You will say the following to them:

"So, for example, Joe, If I said 'fifteen cents' you would simply say 'Nickel, nickel, nickel'. Do you understand how the test is supposed to work?"

Once they acknowledge that they understand, you simply say to them:

"How would you do twenty cents?"

Their reply should be:

"Dime, nickel, nickel."

So far so good. Just a quick note. It may not make any sense (no pun) why we are doing this. It may seem overly simplistic. Trust me, it gets better real soon.

Next, ask them:

"How would you do twenty-five cents?"

Their reply should be:

"Dime, dime, nickel."

Next, ask them:

"How would you do <u>thirty</u> cents?"

Their reply should be:

"Dime, dime, dime."

Now it gets interesting. This is the first time where average people need more than two seconds to divine the answer.

Ask them:

"How would you do <u>thirty-five</u> cents?"

Their reply should be:

"Quarter, nickel, nickel."

Ask them:

"How would you do <u>forty</u> cents?"

Their reply should be:

"Quarter, dime, nickel."

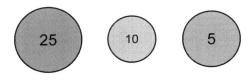

Ask them:

"How would you do <u>forty-five</u> cents?"

Their reply should be:

"Quarter, dime, dime."

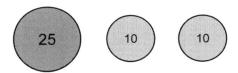

Ask them:

"How would you do <u>fifty</u> cents?"

When you ask them this question, keep calm and act natural. It is not possible to do fifty cents with three coins. You are waiting for them to tell you that it can't be done.

I limit the time on this to thirty seconds, but I do not tell them about the time limit. Usually the real superstars figure this out in less than ten seconds.

There are four possibilities with this question:

1. They give up.
2. They keep trying to figure it out.
3. They get it right away.
4. They get it, but it takes them forever.

Of these, only the third option is acceptable. Do not go easy on this just because you like the candidate. If they get it but it took 45 seconds, trust me, they might be "good" but not "elite". You really want elite. Trust the process. It works if you strictly adhere to it.

What the Coin Test is Testing

The Coin Test is testing if a developer can tell when something is impossible. This may seem wicked, but it isn't. It is not a trick question. Well, it is, but that's okay. A sharp individual will see right through it right away. They will usually say something like, "It can't be done" confidently within a few seconds.

That is the person that you want. Why is this? Because when it comes to designing high end sophisticated software a developer is going to be faced with requirement after requirement that may or may not be possible.

Why the Coin Test is So Important

In the software arena, there are several abilities that are necessary. One of the most important of these is the ability to assess a requirement and determine, both quickly and accurately, if the request is possible. You can easily imagine how bad it would be to promise delivery on a requirement, and then realize after the fact that it is not possible.

Your company runs the risk of upsetting a client and/or having to deal with a truckload of unbillable hours. Trying making money doing that long term.

29

If the developer cannot see through the "fog" and determine right away whether a requirement is possible, your client will lose confidence. That is the worst-case scenario when the client thinks that your developer is incompetent.

Having a developer that can truly problem solve and see when something isn't doable is *just as important,* if not *more important,* than simply figuring out how to code something.

Closely related to this scenario is a more probable situation, where a requirement may be *doable,* however it may not be *desirable,* because the development cost may be much higher than what the client would be willing to pay.

Software developers must have the ability to assess if a requirement is possible. This is true not only if they are talking directly to a client in a small company, or if they are talking to a middle man, like a sales rep or a project manager. (Think of the movie *Office Space*).

> *"Having a developer that can truly problem solve and see when something isn't doable is just as important, if not more important, than simply figuring out how to code something."*

Having developers that can do this for you without having to be held by the hand will pay you dividends many times over. You are probably already nodding your head in agreement with this idea.

One for the Ladies

An interesting note for the ladies - The coin test has shed some light on an interesting fact.

It flies in the face of what many of my fellow programmers, who happen to be guys, would argue. They seem to be under the spell that men are naturally and undeniably better programmers because they tend to be more logical.

I must say in defense of woman that my twenty-five years of research does not seem to agree with this prejudice held by some men.

In fact, the top three people to ever pass the coin test were all women. By "top" I mean they all said "It can't be done" the quickest. The quickest did it in less than two seconds, the third came in at three seconds. (Sorry JO, RW, JC and EW!)

Guys, even the fastest of the fast, take at least five seconds. It might be because we are mentally checking our findings several times, which is fine, however, woman figure this puzzle out faster. The results are hard to dispute.

Alrighty then, let's move on to the second test.

Dave Merton

Chapter 3 – *The Dice Test*

This chapter is going to be broken down into three logical sections, just like the previous chapter. This is a quick listing of the three sections:

1. How to administer the *Dice Test*
2. What the *Dice Test* is testing
3. Why the *Dice Test* is important

Each section will be covered below in more detail.

How to Administer the Dice Test

Before lunging into the Dice Test, you need to do some prep work. It might seem highly unlikely that someone would be unfamiliar with a pair of playing dice. However, you might just come across a few folks that are less familiar with dice specifics than you are.

Now, this could seem strange, especially if you've spent a good chunk of your childhood years playing *Monopoly* and other interesting board games. Just bear in mind, some people will know what dice are, but they may not intimately realize that the sides are numbered from 1 to 6 like in the diagram below:

Make sure that the person being tested is fully aware of the layout of the dice. This is critical to them completing this test successfully.

Okay, now for the test...

Ask the person the following question:

"If I were to shake a pair of dice and then roll them both onto the table, and then add the values together from the two dice, what are the odds that I would roll a total of 'three'?"

That's it! Your part is done. Now you just need to sit back and watch. – That was easy, right?

Note – The person being tested will almost always repeat the question that you just asked. This is normal.

They might even ask you refining questions. Go ahead and answer their questions, but don't give them any hints.

Technically, they shouldn't need to ask any refining questions, because the requirement was straightforward; However, I would never criticize a developer for asking follow up questions on requirements, as this is a good practice.

Note – It's okay if they ask you for a sheet of paper, that's normal. It's no indication of problem solving ability.

For me, it is reassuring to see someone put their thoughts to paper. I believe that this can be very helpful to the problem-solving process.

Now, I need to mention that more people get this test wrong than you would think. Don't be surprised by this.

Also, you need to trust the test. If someone fails the Dice Test then it is a sad but accurate indication that they are lacking a skill in a specific problem-solving dimension. This dimension of problem-solving will be covered in detail later in this chapter.

Note – No amount of other skills can make up for a lack of skill in this problem-solving dimension.

The correct answer is <u>one in eighteen</u>. They might also say <u>two in thirty-six,</u> which is the same thing. Either answer is fine, I just like "one in eighteen" better because I am fastidious and tend to be a stickler on reducing things to "lowest terms".

How do we know that one in eighteen is correct? The next section will cover that in detail.

How We Arrive at the Correct Answer

The math on this is simple. It is statistical in nature. This math is the same math that every casino on Earth uses to figure out odds, so that they can then mathematically proceed to rip everyone off. Casinos make money every minute of every day, so the math must be correct. All those casinos can't be wrong.

What you need to do is figure out how many total combinations there are when you roll a pair of dice. Now what gets confusing is that people somehow get blindsided by this problem and start falling in love with the number twelve. Twelve has nothing to do with this problem.

If it helps, pretend that instead of numbers, the dice have letters on them, or pictures of ugly farmers.

When you roll a single die, no matter what is one the six sides, each side has a one in six chance of landing on top. Therefore, there are six possibilities of what can happen when you roll a single die. Just like there are only two possibilities of what can happen when you flip a coin. The pictures (heads, tails, buffalos, etc.) are irrelevant.

How many combinations do you think there are when you roll two dice simultaneously? It's not twelve, don't fall in love with the number twelve. That's a disease.

When you roll the two dice, there are thirty-six possible combinations of what can happen. Now, mind you, we are not saying how many different 'combined totals' are possible, but how many different actual combinations exist between die 'A' and die 'B'. It is thirty-six different combinations because it is really:

$$6 * 6$$

Refer to the grid below:

	1	2	3	4	5	6
1	1, 1	1, 2	1, 3	1, 4	1, 5	1, 6
2	2, 1	2, 2	2, 3	2, 4	2, 5	2, 6
3	3, 1	3, 2	3, 3	3, 4	3, 5	3, 6
4	4, 1	4, 2	4, 3	4, 4	4, 5	4, 6
5	5, 1	5, 2	5, 3	5, 4	5, 5	5, 6
6	6, 1	6, 2	6, 3	6, 4	6, 5	6, 6

The dice images on the left of the grid represent the six different possibilities for die A.

The dice images on the top of the grid represent the six different possibilities for die B.

The grid itself represents all the joint combinations between the two dice.

Notice that while there is only one possible way to roll 'snake eyes' (one and one, totaling two), there are actually two ways to roll a total of three (one and two, two and one):

	1	2	3	4	5	6
1	1, 1	1, 2	1, 3	1, 4	1, 5	1, 6
2	2, 1	2, 2	2, 3	2, 4	2, 5	2, 6
3	3, 1	3, 2	3, 3	3, 4	3, 5	3, 6
4	4, 1	4, 2	4, 3	4, 4	4, 5	4, 6
5	5, 1	5, 2	5, 3	5, 4	5, 5	5, 6
6	6, 1	6, 2	6, 3	6, 4	6, 5	6, 6

What this tells us is that while there are ultimately thirty-six different combinations, only two of them result in a total of three. Therefore, the odds of rolling a total of three, with two dice, is: <u>two in thirty-six</u>, or more neatly: <u>one in eighteen</u>.

Once you know how this works you can figure out the odds of rolling any other total.

For a total of five there exist four possibilities:

	1	2	3	4	5	6
1	1, 1	1, 2	1, 3	1, 4	1, 5	1, 6
2	2, 1	2, 2	2, 3	2, 4	2, 5	2, 6
3	3, 1	3, 2	3, 3	3, 4	3, 5	3, 6
4	4, 1	4, 2	4, 3	4, 4	4, 5	4, 6
5	5, 1	5, 2	5, 3	5, 4	5, 5	5, 6
6	6, 1	6, 2	6, 3	6, 4	6, 5	6, 6

That means that the odds of rolling a five are twice as great as the odds of rolling a three. The odds of rolling a five are four in thirty-six, or one in nine.

What the Dice Test is Testing

The Dice Test tests whether a developer can *figure out how to figure something out*. In other words, it reveals if an individual can come up, on their own, with a methodology for solving a problem.

Why is this so important? Because in this great big world of software development you must be able to figure out *how* to figure things out *all the time*.

If a developer cannot problem solve in this dimension both quickly and independently, then the developer is not truly qualified to be in the field of software development.

An example of figuring out how to figure something out may be helpful. Let's discuss something that we are all familiar with. We will discuss the conversion of degrees Fahrenheit into degrees Celsius in the section below.

Example - Figuring Out How to Figure Something Out – Converting Degrees Fahrenheit to Degrees Celsius

Imagine that you give someone the formula for converting Fahrenheit to Celsius:

$$C = (F - 32) * 5 / 9$$

Then you ask them to convert a list of Fahrenheit values to Celsius. Could the individual do it? Of course they could, who couldn't? The problem solving has already been done for them, because you would have already provided them with the formula!

Now, just imagine that you ask them to convert a list of Fahrenheit values to Celsius, but you did *not* give them the formula. We will also suppose, for the sake of this example, that they did not already *know* the formula, because they lived on a deserted island. Thus, they never had even heard about either Fahrenheit and/or Celsius.

The only things that you tell them are that:

Water boils at:
    1. 212° Fahrenheit
    2. 100° Celsius.

Water freezes at:
    1. 32° Fahrenheit
    2. 0° Celsius.

From these two bare bones pieces of information that have been provided, there is enough information to cobble together the formula. This is because all that you really need to know are the following two distinct pieces of information:

1. The two units of measure, ° Fahrenheit and ° Celsius, are disproportionate in size. There are 1.8 degrees of Fahrenheit for every 1 degree of Celsius.
2. There is an offset between the two scales of 32° Fahrenheit, from the starting point of water freezing.

From these two pieces of information a person who is a skilled software developer should be able to easily formulate the formula (no pun) in their head.

Did that last statement sound unreasonable? I don't believe that it is unreasonable.

I figured this formula out this when I was ten years old. I thought it was logical and easy. I figured out *how* to figure it out, by developing the formula first (problem solving) and then using it later to convert various degree values of Fahrenheit into the corresponding degree values of Celsius (grunt work).

Why the Dice Test is So Important

In the software world, there are always new problems that need to be solved. These problems can range anywhere from trying to merge data from two different systems where the underlying database schemas are completely different and comparatively de-normalized, to a random question from a client that starts with, "Could the system do this …?"

Software developers must constantly solve problems, and this inevitably includes being forced to figure out *how* to figure things out. Most of the time, there will not be anyone else looking over the software developer's shoulder, whispering the solution into their ear. The solution must come from them directly.

So, let's think about this logically… If a potential software development candidate can't figure out the odds of rolling a (total of) three with two dice, then how will they *ever* be able to size up two separate database systems and then figure out how to seamlessly get the two systems integrated enough to talk to each other properly?

Furthermore, how could this person possibly be on the phone with a client and then field a real-time question about a complicated requirement change where the developer would need to:

1. Visualize the requirements (after understanding what is meant, not just what is being said)
2. Comprehend the client's current workflow
3. Understand how the database will be impacted by this change

… when they couldn't even figure out the odds of rolling a three?

They couldn't. Not a chance.

In both scenarios described above the developer lacking the *figure-out-how-to-figure-things-out* gene would never be able to keep up with these real-world issues. It would be too overwhelming.

Truly skilled and effective software developers need to be able to *hear, see, assess, digest, process, understand, internalize, problem-solve, implement, document, deliver, install, train* and *support* customer requirements. These processes all involve serious problem solving skills. Developers must be able to figure out how to figure things out. It is a critical skill. It is a *must-have* skill.

The Dice Test is a great tool for evaluating an individual in the *figuring-out-how-to-figure-things-out* dimension. It's a great touchstone because either people can solve the Dice Test problem or they can't.

The Dice Test is a fantastic barometer, and it is so quick and easy to use.

Chapter 4 – *The Tic-Tac-Toe Test*

This chapter is going to be broken down into three logical sections, just like the previous two chapters. This is a quick listing of the three sections:

1. How to administer the *Tic-Tac-Toe Test*
2. What the *Tic-Tac-Toe Test* is testing
3. Why the *Tic-Tac-Toe Test* is relevant

We will now cover each section in more detail below.

How to Administer the Tic-Tac-Toe Test

Before we begin, there is something that needs to be mentioned. As with the Dice Test, it is a good idea to make sure that the person that you will be questioning is already familiar with the game Tic-Tac-Toe, and that they fully understand how it works.

The example below shows player "X" winning with three across on the middle row.

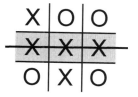

Okay, now for the test...

Ask the person the following question:

"What is the greatest number of X's that I can place onto a Tic-Tac-Toe board __without__ getting Tic-Tac-Toe?"

Note – Sometimes you need to explain that there are no O's on the board, just X's.

You might also let the candidate know that you are actually testing for two things here:

1. What it the greatest number of X's that can be placed?
2. What are the actual positions of the X's?

What's trickier about this test than the previous two is that the person is trying to solve for two things, not just one, so the number of X's is really an unknown.

With the Coin Test either it was doable or not.

With the Dice Test either they figured it out or they didn't, but if they did figure it out, they knew for sure that they had the correct answer.

The Tic-Tac-Toe Test lacks an aspect of certainty from a developer's point of view, since they may come up with a solution, but it still may not be with the greatest possible number of X's.

Note – If they ask you for paper that's okay. They always ask for a new sheet.

Just so you know, the most popular answer to this question is five.

	X	
X		X
X		X

Five is not correct. You can actually fit a total of six X's onto the board. Five in this test is similar to twelve in the Dice Test

There are technically two ways to do it, they are simply mirror images of each other. Either way is fine:

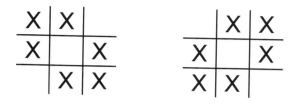

We will cover what this test is all about and why this is an important test in the next few sections; However, I want to just stop for a minute and make a point: This test is not a show stopper if someone doesn't get the *Tic-Tac-Toe Test*.

All I really care about is whether the person solved the first two tests: *The Coin Test* and *The Dice Test*. If they could handle those two tests, then I would offer them a job and put them to work without hesitation.

The *Tic-Tac-Toe Test* is more exploratory than it is defining.

What the Tic-Tac-Toe Test is Testing

The *Tic-Tac-Toe Test* tests whether a developer can *figure something out when there is no clear logical way to approach a problem*. Another way of saying this is that it tests whether a developer can tap into their sub-conscious mind (for more fire power) and then actually listen to their sub-conscious.

Note – By definition, the software developer will be unaware that this (tapping their subconscious) is even happening, it just happens.

It is my theory that their subconscious is getting speed-dialed.

My "theory" is not without solid reasons. I will cover these reasons in the next section.

Why the Tic-Tac-Toe Test is Relevant

You may have noticed that there is no real 'logical' way to figure out the Tic-Tac-Toe Test, unless you approach it 'binarily', but that would take forever, and no one wants to do that approach when they are under the gun in an interview setting.

I also know that no one attempts to do it binarily because, first of all, very few people make it to the third test, and even fewer actually pass it. Of these few elites that solve it, I have a unique perspective as I am observing them. I see what they do, and it's mostly mental, not physical.

A binary approach would require several sheets of paper. No one ever has ever asked for more than the one sheet of paper, or maybe two.

What I have witnessed, every time, is this: The persons who solve it all initially start out by drawing a few X's onto the Tic-Tac-Toe board, but then they put the pencil down and push the paper away.

Next, without fail, they all sit back and think about the problem. Usually about ten seconds later they shout out enthusiastically:

"IT'S SIX!"

...and then they grab the paper, scribble in the six X's correctly and then they hand me the paper.

It is a rush to learn that the person that came in to see you is truly elite, because it is rare. It's like finding treasure.

If you come across a person like this, you *hire* them.

...

I've asked each of them how they finally came to the answer and unanimously they have all confessed that they knew it couldn't be five, because that was too easy. Then, after a few seconds of thinking about it, the answer just "came to them".

You might want to call this intuition, but I look at this as if their subconscious mind (a powerhouse of problem solving energy) whispers the solution into their ear, so to speak.

These few problem solvers are truly elite because when their subconscious mind offers up a timely solution, they know when to listen.

If someone can occasionally tap into that vast resource known as their subconscious mind, then, I believe, there are no problems in this world that will be too impossible for them to solve.

Hire them.

Summary

Congratulations! You did it! You finished this course on evaluating a person's potential for problem solving in three crucial dimensions.

Are you excited? Are you eager to try out your new-found skills? You should be, because you now possess a very *competitive* edge over any of your competition that does not have this training. Your screening process has taken a *quantum leap* forward by comparison.

While these tests will assist you in identifying those who can problem solve and those who cannot problem solve, it cannot tell you many other things about an individual.

For example, these tests cannot tell you who will have a *good work ethic*. Nor can these tests reveal who will *show up to work on time*.

I can absolutely guarantee you that these tests, if properly administered, will (with 100% certainty) identify who out there has the best mental resources for *problem solving*. These tests will also weed out all the folks who cannot problem solve.

I wish you the best in your journey.

In conclusion, I'd like to thank you for taking the time to read this book, and *thank you* for placing your *trust* in me. I'd certainly love to hear your feedback and success stories.

Please leave me a note on Amazon and let me know how much your firm has benefitted from this information.

Thank You,

Dave Merton

Dave Merton

About the Author

Dave Merton has been writing custom software since the mid 1990's. He has written applications for the PC, Web and Smart Phone & tablet devices.

He's done everything from really big to really small; he's consulted for drug companies as well as tutored individuals in software one on one. He's created custom software for testing laboratories (LIMS) as well as worked on web hedging software for oil companies as well as code for the gigantic direct mail industry.

Over those many years, he has developed the methodology in this book for identifying the folks who really and truly know how to problem solve.

Dave has also taught all the following classes publicly, to give something back: Intro to Visual Basic, Microsoft Access, Intro to JavaScript.

When Dave isn't programming he likes to work in the garden, do volunteer work, play with his Cat, read books and invent games.

Manufactured by Amazon.ca
Bolton, ON